THE POWER OF INSPIRATION

Cover source images from Photogear,
Image Club Graphics

Assembled by Marlene Rimler

Cover Design by Todd Kelsey

Published by
Great Quotations Publishing Co.,
Glendale Heights, IL

ISBN 1-56245-214-2

Printed in Hong Kong

ATTITUDE

Attitude is the key to success or failure in most of life's endeavors. Our attitude is not determined by circumstances, but by how we respond to circumstances. You have the capacity to change attitude. Use your power to select quotations that will reinforce the attitudes you want to help mold, inspire, and help you be all the best that you can be.

No life is so hard that you can't make it easier by the way you take it.

Ellen Glasgow

If...I have lost every other friend on earth, I shall at least have one friend left, and that friend shall be down inside of me.

Abraham Lincoln

Your living is determined
not so much by what life
brings to you as by the
attitude you bring to life;
not so much by what
happens to you as by the
way your mind looks at
what happens.

John Homer Miller

The great composer does
not set to work because he
is inspired, but becomes
inspired because he is
working.

Ernest Newman

It is one of the most beautiful compensations of this life that no man can sincerely try to help another without helping himself.

> Ralph Waldo Emerson

You cannot always control circumstances. But you can control your own thoughts.

> Charles E. Popplestone

Things turn out best for the people who make the best of the way things turn out.

> John Wooden

It is understanding that gives us an ability to have peace. When we understand the other fellow's viewpoint, and he understands ours.

Harry S. Truman

We realize that what we are accomplishing is a drop in the ocean. But if this drop were not in the ocean, it would be missed.

Mother Teresa

A mind always employed is always happy. This is the true secret, the grand recipe for felicity.

Thomas Jefferson

A man's worth is no greater than the worth of his ambitions.

Marcus Aurelius

Ambition can creep as well as soar.

Edmund Burke

Caring is a reflex. Someone
slips, your arm goes out. A
car is in a ditch, you join
the others and push. A
colleague at work has the
blues, you let her know you
care. It all comes natural
and appropriate. You live,
you help.

Ram Dass

Give to the world the best
you have, and the best will
come back to you.

Madeleine Bridges

Change your thoughts, and you change your world.

> Norman Vincent Peale

Like the waves of the sea are the ways of fate as we voyage thru life. 'Tis the set of the soul which decides its goal and not the calm or the strife.

> Ella Wheeler Wilcox

True friendship is a plant of
slow growth, and must
undergo and withstand the
shocks of adversity before
it is entitled to the
appellation.

George Washington

Human beings, by changing
the inner attitudes of their
minds, can change the
outer aspects of their lives.

William James

Whenever a man does the best he can, then that is all he can do...

Harry S. Truman

Your living is determined not so much by what life brings to you as by the attitude you bring to life.

John Homer Miller

Positive thinking is reacting positively to a negative situation.

Bill Havens

Far and away the best prize that life offers is the chance to work hard at work worth doing.

Theodore Roosevelt

When you come right down
to it, the secret of having it
all is loving it all.

Dr. Joyce Brothers

The most beautiful thing in
the world is, precisely, the
conjunction of learning and
inspiration.

Wanda Landowska

All things are possible until
they are proved impossible -
even the impossible may
only be so, as of now.

Pearl S. Buck

Take each day as you find it,

If things go wrong, don't
mind it,

For each day leaves behind it,

A chance to start anew.

Gertrude Ellgas

I discovered I always have choices and sometimes it's only a choice of attitude.

Judith M. Knowlton

If you think you are beaten,
you are,
If you think that you dare not,
you don't,
If you'd like to win, but you
think you can't,
It's almost certain you won't.

Anonymous

ENTHUSIASM

It seems very natural when one radiates enthusiasm they are going to be able to do something to inspire others to do something great as well. Thus, quotations about enthusiasm are designed to help you to inspire, to arouse, to elevate and to communicate life within. Enthusiasm reflects caring. To be caring, to be enthusiastic, one can't be around people with those qualities and not catch some of their spirit.

A mediocre idea that generates enthusiasm will go further than a great idea that inspires no one.

Mary Kay Ash

I do the very best I know how; the very best I can; and I mean to keep on doing so; until the end.

Abraham Lincoln

Like simplicity and candor, and other much commended qualities, enthusiasm is charming until we meet it face to face, and cannot escape from its charm.

Agnes Repplier

Enthusiasm is like a ripple in the water...it spreads.

Unknown

Jump into the middle of
things, get your hands dirty,
fall flat on your face, and then
reach for the stars.

Joan L. Curcio

Nothing splendid has ever
been achieved except by those
who dared believe that
something inside them was
superior to circumstance.

Bruce Barton

When you reach for the stars,
you may not quite get one,
but you won't come up with a
handful of mud either.

Leo Burnett

Think of yourself as on the
threshold of unparalleled
success. A whole clear,
glorious life lies before you.

Andrew Carnegie

When you are aspiring to the highest place, it is honorable to reach the second or even the third rank.

Cicero

Whenever you are to do a thing, though it can never be known but to yourself, ask yourself how you would act were all the world looking at you, and act accordingly.

Thomas Jefferson

Go as far as you can see, and when you get there you will see farther.

Orison Sweet Marden

Love the moment, and the energy of that moment will spread beyond all boundaries.

Corita Kent

Again and again, when the struggle seems hopeless and all opportunity lost, some man or woman with a little more courage, a little more effort, brings victory.

James F. Bell

Make opportunities happen.

Mary Kay Ash

Every day's a kick!

Oprah Winfrey

The best jobs haven't been started. The best work hasn't been done.

Berton Braley

You need to get up in the morning and say, "Boy, I'm going to, in my own stupid way, save the world today."

Carol Bellamy

You must learn day by day, year by year, to broaden your horizon. The more things you love, the more you are interested in, the more you enjoy, the more you are indignant about, the more you have left when anything happens.

Ethel Barrymore

Happiness depends upon ourselves.

Aristotle

Happiness is a habit - cultivate it.

Elbert Hubbard

I say if it's going to be done, let's do it. Let's not put it in the hands of fate. Let's not put it in the hands of someone who doesn't know me. I know me best. Then take a breath and go ahead.

Anita Baker

It takes a certain level of aspiration before one can take advantage of opportunities that are clearly offered.

Michael Harrington

GOALS

We must know where we are going before we get there. Too often we get caught up in the daily activities of life and lose sight of what is really important. We rarely stop and actually consider life. Quotations about goals approach life from every perspective, they are meant to focus the mind and stir the soul or perhaps, give you a jolt of reality or of inspiration.

Nothing can stop the man
with the right mental
attitude from achieving his
goal; nothing on earth can
help the man with the
wrong mental attitude.

Thomas Jefferson

If you can see yourself in
possession of your goal, it's
half yours.

Tom Hopkins

Live your life each day as you would climb a mountain. An occasional glance toward the summit keeps the goal in mind, but many beautiful scenes are to be observed from each new vantage point. Climb slowly, steadily, enjoying each passing moment; and the view from the summit will serve as a fitting climax for the journey.

Harold V. Melchert

Within our dreams and aspirations we find opportunities.

        Sue Atchley Ebaugh

If your goals are clear, you can achieve them without fuss.

        Lao-tzu

I will prepare and some day my chance will come.

        Abraham Lincoln

Associate yourself with men of good quality if you esteem your own reputation, for 'tis better to be alone than in bad company.

George Washington

Obstacles are those frightful things you see when you take your eyes off the goal.

Hannah More

We are what and where we are because we have first imagined it....

Donald Curtis

The person who makes a success of living is the one who sees his goal steadily and aims at it unswervingly.

Cecil B. DeMille

To will is to select a goal, determine a course of action that will bring one to that goal, and then hold to that action until the goal is reached. The key is action.

Michael Hanson

My greatest inspiration is a challenge to attempt the impossible.

Albert A. Michelson

Just don't give up trying to do what you really want to do. Where there is love and inspiration, I don't think you can go wrong.

Ella Fitzgerald

In any moment of decision the best thing you can so is the right thing, the next best thing is the wrong thing, and the worst thing you can so is nothing.

Theodore Roosevelt

MOTIVATION

We are motivated to the degree that the decisions we make are our decisions. To know what we really want is the key to motivation. In using motivational quotations to inspire and to lead others you will find that, more often than not, you will always be among the motivated.

Every worthwhile accomplishment, big or little, has its stages of drudgery and triumph; a beginning, a struggle, and a victory.

Abraham Lincoln

Do not follow where the path may lead. Go instead where there is no path and leave a trail.

Unknown

Get action. Do things; be sane, don't fritter away your time...take a place wherever you are and be somebody; get action.

Theodore Roosevelt

You have to know what's important and what's unimportant, for you.

David Harold Fink

The longest journey
Is the journey inwards.
Of him who has chosen his
destiny,
Who has started upon his
quest
For the source of his being.

Dag Hammarskjold

If one advances confidently in
the direction of their dreams,
and endeavors to lead a life
which they had imagined, they
will meet with a success
unexpected in common hours.

Henry David Thoreau

Identify your aim. Choose what you want to do. Base your decision on the truth.

Peter Nivio Zarlenga

We confide in our strength, without boasting of it; we respect that of others, without fearing it.

Thomas Jefferson

You will live your life secure in that you are no longer manipulated by what other people want you to do and be, but are directed by your own inner desires.

H. Stanley Judd

A determination to succeed is the only way to succeed.

William Feather

If the world is cold, make it your business to build fires.

Horace Traubel

I think it's the end of progress if you stand still and think of what you've done in the past. I keep on.

Leslie Caron

Inhabit ourselves that we may indeed do what we want to do.

Mary Caroline Richards

It's so hard when I have to,
and so easy when I want to.

Sondra Anice Barnes

The inner thought coming
from the heart represents the
real motives and desires.
These are the causes of action.

Raymond Holliwell

Need and struggle are what
excite and inspire us.

William James

Nothing contributes so much
to tranquilize the mind as a
steady purpose, a point on
which the soul may fix its
intellectual eye.

Mary Shelley

Do more than exist,

                    LIVE.

Do more than touch,

                    FEEL.

Do more than look,

                    OBSERVE.

Do more than read,

                    ABSORB.

Do more than hear,

                    LISTEN.

Do more than listen,

                    UNDERSTAND.

Do more than think,

                    PONDER.

Do more than talk,

                    SAY SOMETHING.

John H. Rhoades

OPTIMISM

To be an optimist is not to deny reality but rather to understand the nature of things as they are and to have the vision and willingness to alter the existing reality in a way that will have a positive outcome. Quotations on optimism can both stimulate and inspire you and leave you with a "can do" attitude and commitment.

The great pleasure in life is doing what people say you cannot do.

Walter Bagehot

Always bear in mind that your own resolution to succeed is more important than any other one thing.

Abraham Lincoln

If we are to achieve we must look for the opportunity in every difficulty instead of the difficulty in every opportunity.

Walter E. Cole

One cannot have wisdom
without living life.

>Dorothy McCall

From a little spark may
burst a mighty flame.

>Dante Alighieri

Life is too short to be
small.

>Benjamin Disraeli

I'm a great believer in luck,
and I find the harder I work
the more I have of it.

>Thomas Jefferson

Faith that the thing can be
done is essential to any
great achievement.

        Thomas N. Carruthers

The people who get on in
this world are the people
who get up and look for the
circumstances they want
and, if they can't find
them, make them.

        George Bernard Shaw

Every man is the architect
of his own fortune.

        Sallust

Yesterday I dared to struggle. Today I dare to win.

Bernadette Devlin

Faith is the virtue of the storm, just as happiness is the virtue of the sunshine.

Ruth Benedict

It's easy enough to be a starter, but are you a sticker too? It's easy enough to begin a job. It's harder to see it through.

Margaret Thatcher

The optimism of a mind is
indefatigable.

> Margery Allingham

Those who bring sunshine
to the lives of others
cannot keep it from
themselves.

> James Barrie

A man's reach should
exceed his grasp...

> Robert Browning

Liberty, when it begins to take root, is a plant of rapid growth.

George Washington

The difficult we do immediately. The impossible takes a little longer.

Slogan of U.S. Armed Services

There are two ways of spreading light: to be the candle or the mirror that reflects it.

Edith Wharton

It generally happens that
assurance keeps an even
pace with ability.

Samuel Johnson

An optimist may see a light
where there is none.

Michel de Saint-Pierre

VISION

Vision is the gift of seeing clearly what may be. A clarity of vision is necessary for success in any endeavor. Quotations from people who are committed to a vision make excellent testimony. Their thoughts clarify both life and action and are meant to focus and inspire.

Cherish your visions and your dreams as they are the children of your soul; the blueprints of your ultimate achievements.

Napoleon Hill

The best thing about the future is that it comes only one day at a time.

Abraham Lincoln

Nothing happens unless first a dream.

Carl Sandburg

The only limits are, as always, those of vision.

James Broughton

Never trouble another for what you can do for yourself.

Thomas Jefferson

Where there is no vision, the people perish...

Bible, Proverbs 29:18

I hope I shall always possess firmness and virtue enough to maintain what I consider the most enviable of all titles, the character of an honest man.

George Washington

Far away there in the sunshine are my highest aspirations. I may not reach them but I can look up and see their beauty, believe in them and try to follow them.

Louisa May Alcott

To come to be you must have a vision of Being, a Dream, a Purpose, a Principle. You will become what your vision is...

Peter Nivio Zarlenga

It may be those who do most, dream most.

Stephen Leacock

The way of the heart is one of compassion and emotional perception. Therefore, it is never appropriate to suppress an emotion, or to disregard what you feel.

Gary Zukav

The reason so many people never get anywhere in life is because, when opportunity knocks, they are out in the backyard looking for four-leaf clovers.

Walter P. Chrysler

When I look into the future, it's so bright it burns my eyes.

Oprah Winfrey

Happiness is not a state to arrive at, but a manner of traveling.

Margaret Lee Runbeck

Any of us can dream, but
seeking vision is always done
not only to heal and fulfill
one's own potential, but also
to learn to use that potential
to serve all our relations.

Brooke Medicine Eagle

God grant me the serenity to
accept the things I cannot
change, the courage to change
the things I can, and the
wisdom to know the
difference.

Reinhold Niebuhr

Better keep yourself clean and bright; you are the window through which you must see the world.

George Bernard Shaw

My role is to be the ultimate inspirer, to dream the ultimate dreams, to see the vision, and to impart that vision to others.

Arnold C. Greenberg

A wise man will make more opportunities than he finds.

Francis Bacon

Cherish your visions and your dreams as they are the children of your soul; the blueprints of your ultimate achievements.

Napoleon Hill

All our dreams can come true, if we have the courage to pursue them.

Walt Disney

Inspiration at its best means breath, and only too frequently means wind.

G. K. Chesterton

The more sand that has escaped from the hourglass of our life, the clearer we should see through it.

Jean Paul Sartre

May you seek after treasures of precious gold, and find them within the hearts of others.

Mary Summer Rain

The future belongs to those
who believe in the beauty of
their dreams.

Eleanor Roosevelt

The hand cannot reach higher
than does the heart.

Orison Swett Marden

Where we go our vision is.

Joseph Murphy

Other Hardcovers by Great Quotations

Ancient Echoes
Behold The Golfer
Bumps in the Road
Chosen Words
Good Lies for Ladies
Great Quotes from
  Great Teachers
Great Women
Just Between Friends
Love Streams

The Essence of Music
The Perfect Brew
The Power of Inspiration
There's No Place Like
  Home
To A Very Special
  Husband
Woman to Woman
Works of Heart

Other Titles by Great Quotations

365 Reasons to Eat
  Chocolate
A Smile Increases Your
  Face Value
Aged To Perfection
Apple A Day
Champion Quotes
Close to Home
Don't Deliberate . . .
  Litigate
Each Day A New
  Beginning
For Mother–A Bouquet of
  Sentiments
Golf Humor
Good Living
I Think My Teacher
  Sleeps At School
Inspirations
Interior Design for Idiots

Money For Nothing
  Tips for Free
Mrs. Murphy's Laws
Mrs. Webster's
  Dictionary
Parenting 101
Quick Tips for Home
  Improvement
Quotes From Great
  Women
Real Estate Agents and
  Their Dirty Little Tricks
Teachers Are First Class
The Dog Ate My Car
  Keys
The Secret Language
  of Men
The Secret Language of
  Women
Thinking of You
What To Tell Children

GREAT QUOTATIONS PUBLISHING
1967 Quincy Court
Glendale Heights, IL 60139-2045
Phone (708) 582-2800, Fax (708) 582-2813